© Developmental Press
The Cultural & Developmental Institute
240 Argo Avenue
San Antonio, Texas 78209

The Cross-Age Mentoring Program (CAMP) for Children with Adolescent Mentors:
Mentor Handbook

Developed by Michael J. Karcher, Ed.D., Ph.D.

Cover photos from CAMP (Columbus, Wisconsin, 1999)
and Velocity (San Antonio, TX 2012) with written consent

ISBN: 978-1718677180

10 9 8 7 6 5 4 3 2 1
Printed in the United States of America

Acknowledgements:

The Columbus, Wisconsin School District; Brad Powell, Rev. Pat Gahan, and The St. Stephen's Episcopal School in Austin, Texas; The Boy with a Ball staff who conduct the "Velocity" program in Harlandale ISD, San Antonio, Texas.

Michael Garringer, Eve McDermott, Patty McCrae, Amy Cannata, and Nicky Martin at the National Mentoring Center, Education Northwest, Portland Oregon.

Special thanks to my editor, co-author and younger brother, Ben Judson

TABLE OF CONTENTS

IMPORTANT NUMBERS   4

INTRODUCTION: DEVELOPMENTAL MENTORING, THE CHALLENGES, IMPROVING   5
    CHANCE ENCOUNTERS, & WHAT'S TO COME

TELEMACHUS   10

TYPES OF MENTORS: CLASSIC, GROUP, FRIEND, PEER (DEVIANCY TRAINING), LONG-TERM 12

PART ONE: THE BASIC DUTIES OF A DEVELOPMENTAL MENTOR

MENTOR RESPONSIBILITIES: FOSTERING GOALS OF PROGRAM, MAINTAINING CONTACT   16
    WITH MENTEE (HELPFUL HINTS), SHARING EXPECTATIONS (HELPFUL HINTS), &   18
    MAINTAINING CONTACT WITH PROGRAM COORDINATORS (NO QUESTION IS TOO SMALL), 20
    AND EXPECTATIONS: THE SHORT LIST   22

MENTORING CONTRACT   23

CRISES SITUATIONS! SUPPORT AND INTERVENTION, DIRECT DISCLOSURE, SUSPECTED   24
    ABUSE, EMERGENCIES

TEN THINGS TO REMEMBER ABOUT MENTORING (AKA KORNELS OF WISDOM)   26

RAPPORT BUILDING: THINGS TO CONSIDER BEFORE MEETING   28

MENTOR-MENTEE TERMINATION RITUAL   29

HOPES & CONCERNS   30

OUR FIRST MEETING: A PLANNING WORKSHEET   33

PART TWO: SHARING YOUR POINTS OF VIEW OR LEARNING YOUR MENTEES ASKING
ASSERTIVELY FOR WHAT YOU WANT (OVERVIEW)   35
FOUR GOALS OF MISBEHAVIOR   35
CONSTRUCTIVE CRITICISM   41

PART THREE: WORKING WITH DIFFERENT POINTS OF VIEW
YOUR STYLE OF CONFLICT RESOLUTION   41
PROBLEM-SOLVING STEPS   45
SOLUTION FOCUSED HELPING   46

PART FOUR: A THEORY TO PULL IT ALL TOGETHER
PERSPECTIVE-TAKING SKILLS   49
THE ANIMALS OF YUMEWII MOUNTAIN   52
SULLIVAN'S STAGES   53
APPENDIX: BEHAVIOR MANAGEMENT TECHNIQUES FOR 1-ON-1 SUPERVISION   54
    PROBLEM BEHAVIORS—EFFECTIVE DISCIPLINE   57
CONNECTEDNESS SCALE, SOCIAL INTEREST SCALE, AND REFERENCES   59

Program Coordinator

Office Phone

Email

Assistant Coordinator, School Liaison, or School Counselor

Office Phone

Email

Lead Mentor(s): ________________ :   ________________ :

Phone   **Phone**

Email   **Email**

Protégé (s):________________ :   ________________ :

Phone   **Phone**

Email   **Email**

Mentee's Family: Parent(s) name(s):

Phone

Email

Name of any of your mentees' siblings (and where they go to school):

Other important numbers or information:

Welcome and Congratulations!
You are embarking on a very rewarding journey. People usually describe their mentoring experiences as some of the most important times in their lives. Being a mentor allows individuals to learn who they are by sharing themselves with others. Being a mentor provides an opportunity to be a special friend, to make an impact on a child's life, and to learn about different types of people. Many mentors find out through mentoring that they have a lot to offer others simply by being genuine with others, by listening, sharing, and caring. Many also discover that they enjoy learning about people, cultures and values other than what they have known.

Developmental Mentoring

The developmental mentoring program is called CAMP, which stands for the Children with Adolescent Mentors' Cross-Age Mentoring Program (CAMP). The CAMP was designed to support elementary and middle school children through a phase in their education and development when many children first experience disconnection from school. This disconnectedness manifests itself in lower grades, increased behavioral disorders, and conflict regarding their attitudes toward school. Addressed quickly enough through the creation of new bonds or connections with same-age and older peers who can model positive school attitudes, supportive peer relationships, and who show children they are cared for, these children can get back on track and begin to enjoy school more.

Mentoring provides children two important ingredients of successful development: supportive relationships and exposure to a variety of activities, people and cultures. The CAMP program mentors try to help promote their mentees' connectedness to school, teachers, peers, reading, family, self and future. The mentoring relationship is central to the effectiveness of the program as a whole. CAMP mentors use their relationship to promote connectedness but also help teach social skills that their mentees can use to forge better relationships with others.

The CAMP program you will be a part of also includes such a summer program and Saturday events, but at its core are the weekly meetings after school between your mentee and you. This weekly mentoring is arguably the most important part of the program. From the beginning of the school year until summer, you will work closely with your mentee in program activities designed to promote the mentees' connectedness to others, society and themselves. Your role as a mentor is to listen, provide support and suggestions, and keep your mentee aware of the importance of school, of being actively involved in a variety of social and academic activities, and to encourage him or her to learn about him or herself, others, and society. You provide the role of big brother/sister, friend, counselor and mentor. The importance of your presence in the life of your mentee cannot be overemphasized. You could change your mentee's life and be someone he or she will remember and talk about for the rest of his or her life.

The Challenge

Being a mentor is challenging. It takes work and commitment. When people have not enjoyed mentoring, there are typically two reasons. First, they may not have invested themselves fully or honestly. Either they couldn't provide sufficient time and energy to the relationship, or they were not honest about feeling disconnected from or unable to reach their mentees. Mentors who find out either (a) that they cannot provide enough energy or time to be a mentor, or (b) that they have a poor relationship with their mentees must let the Program Coordinators know immediately so that they can help get things back on track, or, on a rare occasion, a re-pairing can take place when necessary.

A second reason mentoring relationships become problematic is that mentors become too concerned about making mistakes or are too worried to ask for help. Most often in this case, the mentors could easily get back on track if they would consult with the program staff and get the support, guidance, or encouragement they need to fulfill their potential as a mentor.

These obstacles are mentioned here not to discourage you from the challenge, but rather to help you think realistically about mentoring. Rest assured, we are confident in your ability to be a great mentor, and we want you to know that we will help you every step of the way.

How will training help me in my "chance encounter" with my mentee?

In an article called *The psychology of chance encounters and life paths*, Albert Bandura (1982)[1] explains the importance of chance encounters in the life paths of individuals, and recommends that we attempt to explain the factors that make chance encounters significant for different people. Bandura suggests there are

---

[1] Bandura, A. (1982). The psychology of chance encounters and life paths. *American Psychologist, 37(7), 747-755.*

three aspects of chance encounters, such as between you and your mentee, that increase the odds that a chance encounter between two individuals will have a long-lasting impact.

First, there has to be some glue to make the passing encounter into a lasting encounter. Somehow, you and your mentee need to see how you are related to each other, learn how you are similar in some way, and find each other interesting. Having shared interests and the ability to communicate them is the first predictor that a positive chance encounters will make a difference. This requires talking, sharing points of view, and telling each other about interests and experiences.

> "If persons are to affiliate with those whom they have had the good or bad fortune to meet, they must posses some of the personal resources needed to gain sufficient acceptance to sustain continued involvement with them." (Albert Bandura, 1982, p. 150)

Invariably there are things that can link individuals—shared interests, histories, backgrounds, goals, etc.—but structured activities may be needed to encourage the back-and-forth exchanges that are necessary to help reveal these links. Bandura calls these "entry skills." People use entry skills to enter into another's life by relating, sharing, and expressing interest in each other. This is where this handbook and its training in perspective-taking skills, assertive communication, and encouragement become helpful to you.

Second, these "links" between you and your mentee need to lead to mutual attraction. After meeting and greeting each other—and we have a special activity just for that—there needs to be something that attracts you two back to each other. We hope that the meet and greet activity sets the stage for this by building on some natural attraction between you both, but this interest in each other has to be cultivated too. Mentors need to actively look for things that make their mentees interesting.

Mentors also need to consider ways they might be interesting and attractive to the mentee, and then remember to bring these things into the relationship. This requires you to try to take your mentee's perspective—that is, to stand in his or her shoes and see how your mentee sees you. For example, what if a mentee is attracted to a mentor because the mentor plays basketball and the mentee wants to too. It is not enough that the mentee knows the mentor has this skill, interest or experience. The mentor needs to play up this by talking about it, telling stories, relating it to the mentee's life in order to help foster the mentee's attraction to the mentor through their shared interest in basketball.

Providing empathy, praise and attention are also ways to foster this attraction. People like people who like them. Listening to your mentee, using reflective listening to convey accurate understanding (or empathic accuracy), and giving sincere praise when your mentee demonstrates efforts or skills that are impressive—all of these foster attraction. Jean Rhodes, an expert on mentoring, suggests "when adolescents develop close connections with mentors, their ability to connect with other adults, especially their parents, also improves" (2002, p. 38). We have found that the CAMP program does indeed improve mentee's relationships with parents, and this improvement in the parent-child relationship partly helps explains improvements in grades and school attitudes that can result from participating in the CAMP program (see CAMP study by Karcher, Davis & Powell, 2002).

How? We think that when children's relationships with their parents improve, the children then are more open to their teacher's influence—as another supportive adult at school. Being more connected to their teachers makes the children work harder in school. We also think that the improved parent relationships result from two things: (a) time the CAMP kids spend with their parents at SuperSaturdays and related events, and (b) the way in which a new, positive, prosocial relationship with an older peer helps the children feel better about the older people in their lives, like their parents and teachers.

A third set of qualities that Bandura suggests make chance encounters into powerful relationships include (1) your self-evaluation of the degree to which you feel you can connect with others, (2) your need for affiliation, closeness, and someone with whom to identify, and (3) the degree to which you have already established a set of values and interests that are compatible with your mentee's.

Both you and your mentee will complete an interest inventory. This might help us in matching you together by your shared interests. It is likely more useful, however, when used as a way for you and your mentee to start a conversation about your shared interests. It may help you remember events from your life that you can share with your mentee that help you two connect.

As one other way to help you assess your similarity with your mentee, you will be able to compare your "connectedness profile" with your mentee's. We have mentors and mentees complete *the Hemingway,* which is a measure of adolescent connectedness, and discuss it with each other as one after school activity. The connectedness survey that you and your mentee both complete can be compared to learn about each other's degree of connectedness to self, others, and society. We also use it to measure changes that result from participating in the program.

What's to come?

In the following sections, you will be walked through a set of activities that will help you practice some of the skills that you will need to form that "mutual attraction" with your mentee. These activities will help you learn how to teach your mentee some social and communication skills as well. Finally, the sections that follow provide the ground rules and set some boundaries to increase the likelihood that your experience is fun, safe, and sustainable.

"Mentoring is the relationship between an older, more experienced mentor and an unrelated, younger protégé. The mentor typically provides ongoing guidance, instruction, and encouragement aimed at developing the competence and character of the protégé. Over the course of the relationship, the mentor and protégée develop a special bond of mutual commitment, respect, and loyalty which facilitates the youth transition into adulthood."

(Rhodes, 1994, p. 188-189)[2]

The primary task of you as a mentor is to be a role model and friend. In so doing you will want to explore the possibilities that the child may have for academic success and show the child how to make the most of them. Hopefully your protégé or "mentee" will walk away from the experience feeling empowered or at least better about him or herself than before the program—before having this "chance encounter" with you. This will happen naturally as you spend time with and interact supportively with your mentee.

The word mentor comes from Greek mythology. First appearing in Homer's *Odyssey*, Mentor was a friend of Odysseus, to whom the king entrusted his household and family when he sailed (Freedman, 1993, p. 31).[3] Specifically Mentor was given the task of safekeeping and helping to facilitate the social and moral development of the king's only son.

(An interesting twist in the story is that the goddess Athena takes on Mentor's appearance and begins to guide, encourage, and prepare the king's son for the life ahead of him. Curious, isn't it? Why would she be needed to help Mentor do his work? What traits or skills might she bring to "Mentoring?" Perhaps there are some essential skills that mentors need (such as listening, encouraging, being empathic, concerned, and supportive) that society may provide girls more practice in than boys. If so, even though boys may bring very unique and important skills to the task of mentoring, this may be a set of skills that some male mentors have to work harder to demonstrate or convey to their mentees? What do you think?)

---

[2] Rhodes, J. E. (1994). Older and wiser: Mentoring relationships in childhood and adolescence. *The Journal of Primary Prevention, 14(3)*, 187-196.
[3] Freedman, M. (1993). *The kindness of strangers: Adult mentors, urban youth, and the new volunteerism.* San Francisco: Jossey-Bass.

This story is particularly interesting in that it suggests that the mentor has a more divine and important purpose than the child expected. The king's son expected to be safeguarded and watched over, but Athena disguised as Mentor has in mind to help prepare the youth for an important future by better helping him to better understanding himself through their relationship. This is key. Athena does her work as Mentor *through* their relationship more than through any advice, instruction, or training she provides. The relationship she creates for him to *grow in* and *grow through* is what makes all the difference.

The word itself stems from several Greek roots meaning "to think, to counsel, to remember, and to endure." These are four important tasks of mentors. Mentors must think about their purpose. They counsel their mentees or protégés. They must *remember*. Mentors must remember their role as a guide, companion, and friend to the youth, and that they must remember their mentees (literally, not forget them) in order to maintain contact with their mentees consistently. This is because for a mentor to be effective, their contact must endure over time. The mentee has to feel he or she can count on the mentor to be there, consistently, reliably. The mentee is well mentored when he or she feels guided, listened to, remembered, and seen regularly over time.

Phillip and Hendry (1996)[4] suggested there were at least five types of mentors. All of these types of mentoring have to do with (a) promoting the mentee's development, (b) helping mentees deal with anxiety resulting from their uncertainty about how to act or what to say in certain situations, and (c) helping mentees achieve their goals. These may be formal, as in "classic mentoring," or informal, like the kind of mentoring best friends provide each other.

1) Classic mentoring:

A more "experienced mentor provides support, advice, and challenge" to a youth or protégé. Their time together may focus on shared interests or hobbies, and the mentor's place is as a role model who recognizes the mentee or protégé as an important or "special person." Here the mentor's role is specifically to teach and to guide the youth in the direction the mentor has gone.

CAMP Mentors are the most like Phillip and Hendry's "classic mentors" because they work with a specific child, and their work is to help the children think about their futures, do better in school, and develop more solid interpersonal relationships and skills.

2) Mentor for a group of individuals:

Here a group of mentees look to an individual or group of individuals for support, advice, or challenge. Examples of this include camp counselors, leaders in girl scouts, or some other organized group with leaders or available mentors for other members to provide support, respect, listening, and understanding. Typically the mentor need not be older, but is seen as having important previous experience in a context or group. And the individual is seen as reliable and "in touch."

CAMP Mentors are like "team mentors" in that they interact with all the kids in the program and look for opportunities to talk with, help them out, and listen to all of them at various times. However, the CAMP mentor's primary focus is on his or her own mentee.

A small number of experienced mentors in the program will be designated as "lead mentors." Lead mentors serve as "mentors to the mentors," offering support and advice, and helping their fellow mentors better understand their job. These lead mentors serve as mentors to the whole group of mentors.

---

[4] Philip, K., & Hendry, L. B. (1996). Young people and mentoring--Towards a typology? *Journal of Adolescence, 19*(3), 189-201.

3) **Friend to Friend mentoring:**
This person provides a "safety net" for the youth, particularly the youth who is mistrustful of adults or who often feels misunderstood by adults. This mentor provides a setting for the youth to share confidential or sensitive information, a place to talk about values, and even a forum to discuss activities before or after they have occurred. This type of mentoring occurs mostly among best friends.

CAMP Mentors are like "Friend" mentors in that they are seen by the mentees as people "who understand me." Mentees feel their mentors will listen to them, take their issues seriously, and won't repeat sensitive things they might share with their mentor. Being an older peer allows you access to your mentee's life in ways adults don't have.

Of course, this does not mean that mentors would withhold important information regarding the mentees' safety or health. Mentors should always ask themselves two sets of questions about the information mentees share with them. First, "If I was this child's parent, would I want to know about this information?" Second, "Does this information tell me that this child could get hurt, is being hurt, or might hurt someone else?" If the mentor's answer is yes to either, they should talk to a Program Coordinator about whether parents should be included in those with whom the child talks about these matters.

4) **Peer group mentoring:**
Like team mentoring, here a group of individuals serve as a collective mentor to a youth. A group of friends who spend time together regularly, talk about important issues, and share advice with each other engage in this mentoring. This type of mentoring is most helpful to youth trying to learn how to "grow up" or to act in certain places, like school, at parties, etc.

CAMP Mentors are like peer group mentors because the mentees look to them for examples of what is appropriate behavior, what is acceptable (e.g., in class or on the bus), and they will model their behavior after their mentors'. This is one of the reasons that we are particularly wary of the teen mentors modeling misbehavior. When mentors goof around with each other, sometimes thinking their mentees' aren't paying attention—though they almost always are — the mentees can get the wrong idea about what is appropriate for someone their age.

For example, a study entitled, "When interventions harm," by Dishion, McCord, and Poulin (1999)[5] increased the community's concerns about the potential negative effects of interventions for youth. They reported that those most vulnerable to "deviancy training" may be those more at risk for engaging in delinquent behavior. Deviancy training is the formal term for the process in which peers undercut the potentially positive influences of conventional, adult-approved activities and experiences by promoting, instead, authority undermining behaviors. For example, imagine if one mentor who is working with her mentee has a conversation with a peer (who is another mentor) about drinking or smoking over the weekend. The mentee hears this and thinks, "Ah, that is what older kids do and think is cool." When this happens, regardless of what structured, prosocial activity the mentor is "trying" to promote in that week's planned activity, what the mentee learns is really more about misbehavior than about the lesson at hand. Peer group mentoring—where you and your peers model prosocial, caring, non-risky behavior—is a challenge, but is it very important you realize your ability to do harm as well as good (or instead of good) if you are not careful about what you model to your mentee as okay behavior.

5) Long term mentoring:

This includes adults who the youth knows through his/her family or community. These might be uncles, neighbors, or older kids at school.

CAMP Mentors may become like this if they spend considerable time with their mentee and if their mentees look to them as trustworthy "elders." However, one thing we have learned is that it is better to plan just a one-year relationship and to plan to wrap-up, close or end the match at the end of the year. Why? First, a good one-year experience with a mentor and an opportunity to practice saying "goodbye" in a constructive fashion is better than the possible benefits of multiple-year match that might happen. Most matches will end after one year regardless. So it is best to make one school year the expectation. However, if both of you return for a second year in the program, and you want to be together again, great.

Like the doctor's Hippocratic oath, it's critical to do no harm. When a kid expects you to be his or her mentor for year upon year, there is a very high chance that he or she will be disappointed. The sadness that results when these expectations are not met could erase all of the positive benefits of your time together. So, while

---

[5] Dishion, T. J., McCord, J., & Poulin, F. (1999). When interventions harm: Peer groups and problem behavior. *American Psychologist, 54,* 755-764.

long-term mentoring is great, it is best considered something that happens naturally in a kid's life outside the program. Think of it this way—after having a good experience with you, your mentee will be better able to find long-term mentors in the real world. You are providing practice for those later experiences or chance encounters.

As a **CAMP** Mentor you may engage in all five types of mentoring, or you may find that one type best reflects your work with your mentee. That will be determined by many things: your and your mentee's personalities, interests, time, commitment, experiences and goals. No two mentoring relationships are the same.

Fostering Goals of the Program
The primary goals of the program are (a) to help connect youth to promising futures as productive members of society and (b) to promote academic success among children so that as teens they are better able to take advantage of opportunities to explore and exploit their innate talents, aptitudes, and interests. To promote school achievement and the skills needed to succeed in life, the program is oriented toward developing meaningful relationships—promoting what we call "connectedness"—between the children and society, others, and their "self."

The program helps children connect to society by strengthening the links between the children and their schools, communities, and their understanding of the possibilities the future might hold for them. It intends to bolster the children's connectedness to others primarily through the development of the mentoring relationship. These relationships can help children better understand themselves in terms of their unique interests and talents, their cultural background, and their developing identities. For this reason, the mentoring relationship provides the program's primary vehicle for change, development, and academic success among the mentees. Given these goals, there are some basic guidelines you need to follow.

Maintaining Contact with Your Mentee

The primary focus of the CAMP Mentoring Program is the ongoing development of the relationship between mentors and mentees. As such, we ask mentors to do three things:

1) Be aware of your own contributions to the relationship. Be planful and thoughtful about activities you would like to do with your mentee, and keep the match alive and fun.
2) Be aware of the progress of the relationship. Pay attention to what your mentee learns and how his or her behavior changes over the year. Share your positive assessments of (your feelings about) the match with your mentee. Also note problems, both your mentee's personal problems and those in your relationship. When you notice problems, seek out program staff support for ideas about how best to support your mentee.
3) Be open to learning about relationships through experiences with your mentee. You can apply what you learn through mentoring for the rest of your life. We

call CAMP "developmental mentoring" because we have found it benefits both you and your mentee. So, watch for changes in both of you.

The role of the mentor is to develop a consistent, supportive, individual relationship with the mentee that focuses on developing the mentee's academic skills and interpersonal interests. As a mentor, you are in a position to see and inspire what your mentee might become. Mentors don't force their mentees to be this way or that way, but help them discover their own unique personalities.

It is very important that the attention and concern you give your mentee is offered consistently. Your mentee needs to be able to count on you being there for them at every meeting. This means that when you make a commitment to meet your mentee for all scheduled activities. It should be your first priority, barring any emergency. Being consistent and accountable will build trust between you and your mentee.

And, think ahead. When you cannot make a meeting or event, try to let your mentee and/or your Program Coordinator know immediately. That way plans can be made by the program staff to be sure a "protégé" is there to work with your mentee in your absence, and your mentee will still feel like you considered him or her even though you could not be there.

Promoting your mentees' self-esteem is one of the goals of the program to. As a mentor, it will be one of your goals to see that the sort of activities you undertake with your mentee, how you undertake them (e.g., do you make all the decisions, or do you empower your mentee to make suggestions too), will work to build your mentee's self-esteem and self-confidence. Self-esteem is built through experiencing success, through receiving praise for one's successes, and from coming to value one's uniqueness. Therefore, your goal should be to provide empathy, praise and attention consistently to your mentee.

(How to stay in contact with the mentee)
⇒ Make, give, or get and send holiday (e.g., birthday) cards. Find out what holidays are special to your mentee and bring a card to the meeting, or make contact with a call. Realize, however, once you call your mentee, you might start to get more calls (than you would like) from your mentee in return.
⇒ Find out when he or she has big events occurring at school or with the family. If you want to visit your mentee at a school or family function, check it out with him or her before going. If you can't attend an important event at which you

are expected, give your mentee a call and wish them luck. Later check in to see how it went.
⇒ If you schedule a regular time to call, be sure to follow through.
⇒ Know your mentee's address and phone number and encourage him or her to let you know if the address or number changes. If you are comfortable doing so, provide your email address so that he or she can write you.

Sharing Expectations

The best mentoring relationships are *reciprocal*—that is, both the mentor and the mentee benefit from their relationship. You should not feel as if you are doing all of the work. It is up to you to encourage your mentee to seek you out and to ask for things that he or she needs. In fact, in one study of the CAMP program, we found that the more the mentee "sought out her mentor's support" the stronger the relationship was (Karcher, Nakkula, and Harris, 2005). Part of your job is to make sure your mentee knows that you are there to respond to his or her needs. Another part is to make your needs known (e.g., that you can talk on the phone Saturday before 7 p.m. if your mentee needs to reach you, but that on Sundays you study), empower your mentee to initiate some of the plans for things you will do, and discuss plans for future activities during the free time in the afternoon meetings. Don't allow your relationship with your mentee to become one-sided, or else you will exhaust yourself by doing all the work, and your mentee will not feel as involved in the relationship.

(Helpful Hints)
⇒ Tell your mentee that all conversations are confidential unless you have reason to believe that he or she is in danger, in which case you'll talk to a parent, Counselor, Principal, or Program Coordinator.
⇒ Do not discuss your mentee and his or her problems publicly.
⇒ Always make promises sparingly and keep them faithfully.
⇒ Maintain consistent and regular attendance to meetings; give your mentee and the Program Coordinators warning if you must miss a meeting.
⇒ Keep an open mind and don't be judgmental.
⇒ Respect each mentee's beliefs and religious habits.
⇒ Do not criticize school (his or yours) or the program. Similarly, don't promote or model other behaviors that parents would disapprove of. Remember, we call this "deviancy training."
⇒ Be sensitive to other people's feelings.

⇒ Don't be too thin-skinned (e.g., easily offended)--realize that a child's teasing or put-downs may reflect bad habits, poor self-esteem, ineffective social skills, their own feelings, ways his or her peers tend to interact, or even his or her clumsy efforts to be cool or close with you.

⇒ Use such situations as opportunities to model effective communication. If your mentee says something inappropriate or offensive, ask why he or she said that. Help your mentee understand how to express those thoughts and feelings in more appropriate ways.

⇒ Enjoy yourself and see what you can learn about your mentee and yourself.

⇒ For birthdays and special holidays, if you choose to spend money on your mentee please try to keep the price under $15.00.

⇒ Never give your mentee any medication.

Remember you are under no obligation to spend your money on your mentee. There is plenty to do that is that is free, and a thoughtful hand-written card or note is better than any gift you would buy. Should you choose to spend your own money make sure that you explain in your own way that this is not a requirement. Often mentees will compare what their mentors give each of them and it can become quite messy and disappointing for the children who receive less. Therefore, the less that is spent on or given to mentees the fewer expectations get set for other matches and fewer will be disappointed as a result.

You will maintain better relationships with the other mentors if you don't give gifts or do things that then their mentees expect them to do. Gifts are the best example of this, but there are others. Just keep in mind that you are part of a program. If you break the rules and invite the child over to your house for an event, other kids will feel less liked by their mentors because they weren't invited over by their mentors. This can become a real problem for everyone.

Maintain Contact with Program Coordinators

During the year, you may find that you need to talk to someone about your mentee, the relationship, or about your work as a mentor. Do not feel that seeking support is a sign that you have done anything wrong. It is your job to seek support anytime you think your match could be going better than it is. You should go first to a lead mentor in your program. Let one of these experienced mentors know about your questions or problems, without betraying the confidence of your mentee. These lead mentors have a lot of experience with the program, and they can usually help clarify things for you. If you are having a problem with your mentee that requires you to talk about specific things he or she said in a meeting, go to the CAMP Coordinator, or your school guidance counselor (if the CAMP Coordinator is not available).

Although your work with your mentee is confidential (that is, private) these adults are your supervisors. That means that, unlike your friends or other adults, you can tell the Program Coordinators and School Counselor about what you and your mentee talk about. They also will keep this material confidential. Their primary role is to provide an ear for you, to help you think through how to handle situations, and to help you feel good about your work.

Don't feel bad for contacting the staff for support. A study of the Big Brothers Big Sisters teen mentoring program (called the High School Bigs program) found that programs where mentors utilized their program staff more for support and ideas had a bigger impact on the mentees (Herrera, et al. 2008).[6] Again, seeking out support is what you are *encouraged to do* not a sign that you have done anything wrong.

You also should share with these adults those experiences that make your mentoring rewarding to you. Let them know how you have been able to connect with your mentee. Talk to the Program Coordinator so that they don't always feel that *they* must be the ones to ask "How's it going with your mentee." Feel free to talk with them in public places about general positive or negative concerns, but remember that you may have private information about your mentee that is best shared in less public places.

---

[6] Herrera, C., Kauh, T. J., Cooney, S. M., Grossman, J. B., & McMaken, J. (2008). *High school students as mentors: Findings from the Big Brothers Big Sisters school-based mentoring impact study*. Philadelphia: Public/ Private Ventures.

Sometimes Principals may wonder if the CAMP program is a good idea. It costs the school money, takes up students' time, and requires lots of support. So program staff are always in need of evidence that the program is going well, even though a recent study of the CAMP program found that CAMP mentors reported greater gains in academic self-esteem and connectedness after serving as mentors (Karcher, 2009). And other studies have shown that it has positive effects on the mentees as well (Karcher, 2005). So, share your good experiences as well as your bad experiences with staff, and never refrain from sharing your ideas about how to improve the program and make it even better. The program is highly structured, but is it "alive" (or "organic") meaning it is meant to grow, develop, and get stronger. One of the best ways to make the program stronger is to get input from the people in the program – you.

Some situations when you might want to contact a Program Coordinator:

- Your mentee tells you something that worries or concerns you.
- Your mentee asks you to do something with them you are unsure about doing.
- You are feeling "over your head" or when things "feel weird" as a mentor.
- You suspect that your mentee is in danger.
- Your relationship with you mentee is strained or difficult.
- You do not like your mentee as much as you used to.
- You feel you cannot continue to work with your mentee.
- You want to know if it is appropriate to involve your mentee's family in dealing with an issue.

No question is too small or too large.
It's better to be safe and ask your program coordinator if you are not sure about something than to wonder .

Now that you have read and thought about the goals of the CAMP Mentoring program and about what a mentor is, ask yourself if you feel you will be able to fulfill your role. If not, then talk to one of the Coordinators or a Counselor. There is no shame in knowing your limits. Problems arise when people commit to relationships they can't honor or maintain. So think about what is asked of you, and be sure you understand it and feel comfortable with it. It is better to wait until you are sure you can handle it and have the time than to have to quit mid-year when you realize you have taken on too much. By that time, your mentee will surely wonder what he or she did to push you away—and you want to avoid that from happening.

Certainly the only way the mentoring relationship will work is if the mentor initiates an effort, tries to maintain and deepen the relationship, and tries to keep the relationship alive. In this section of the Mentor Handbook and in the training we have discussed a number of things we expect from mentors. These are all important to your ability to effectively initiate, deepen and maintain your mentoring relationship. As a mentor you agree to fulfill these expectations. If you are not able to fulfill the expectations, then you may be asked to give your mentee to someone else.

But we are sure you will find that being accountable to a child who very much wants your friendship is a worthwhile and rewarding endeavor. Your reward will come from the relationship you develop with your mentee.

Keep in mind that it is always okay and good to talk to the lead mentors and coordinator when things are not working out--this is better than simply abandoning a child, particularly if it is a child for whom abandonment is not a new experience. It can be emotionally very painful to children when they feel they have been forgotten, rejected or abandoned without an explanation. We've even found that when mentors are inconsistent—miss meetings—their mentees can come to feel less attractive and report lower self-esteem (Karcher, 2005). So invest yourself and give it your all. If you feel it is not working out, talk to someone.

Expectations: The Short List
- To engage in your mentoring relationship with an open mind.
- To attend all scheduled program activities: after school, Super Saturdays, and the two weeks of summer program.
- To be on time.
- To notify the Program Coordinator (and your mentee when possible) if an emergency arises that prevents you from attending an activity.
- To keep discussions with your mentee confidential, except in cases where you are concerned about the safety of your mentee.
- To notify Program Coordinator of any emergency situations and any situations or events that you need help handling.
- To notify the Program Coordinator if there is a change in your relationship with your mentee.

Mentoring Contract

As a mentor I agree to the following:

1) I will spend time getting to know my mentee, while offering empathy, praise and attention.
2) I will have fun and know my job is not to be a tutor, coach or parent.
3) I will attend summer activities (unless I arrange in advance with the Coordinator not to participate in the summer events).
4) I will attend Super Saturdays
5) I will contact a Program Coordinator or Guidance Counselor should a problem occur for me or my mentee.
6) I will tell the Program Coordinator before any meetings I know I must miss.
7) I will notify the Program Coordinator, as soon as possible, if I or my mentee don't feel that there is a good fit between us.
8) I will attend and participate in all trainings (and bring this handbook).
9) I will conduct the "termination" or closure ritual at the end of the year.

In return you may expect from the Program and the Coordinator(s) :

10) The Program will provide you mentor training.
11) The Program will provide you frequent group supervision (check-ins) throughout the school year, often over lunch.
12) The Program will provide you unlimited individual supervision during the school year in person, by request, and as needed (via the phone or email).
13) The Program will provide you the opportunity to impact someone else's life and grow personally in the process.

____________________   _____________

Mentor's Signature   Date

____

Mentor's Printed Name

CRISIS SITUATIONS!

As a CAMP Mentor, you are responsible for contacting one of the Program Coordinators immediately in any type of crisis situation regarding your match. The following are examples of situations in which mentors should ask for help immediately.

- Your mentee begins to talk about life not being worthwhile, appears depressed (looks sad, lacks energy, grades have dropped, cries easily), or talks openly about suicide;
- Your mentee threatens to harm someone else;
- Your mentee mentions being either physically or sexually abused;
- Your mentee begins to "act strange," talks without making sense, or mentions hearing or seeing things that are not there.

Support and Intervention

If your mentee tells you that she or he feels unsafe or has been abused or neglected by a parent, neighbor, relative, friend, or stranger, it is important that you listen carefully and take very seriously the nature of the disclosure. Here are some guidelines for handling conversations in which children disclose such information.

Direct Disclosure:

In cases where your mentee directly discloses to you that she or he is being abused or mistreated in any way, **it is important to:**

- Stay calm and listen. If you stay calm, this will help your mentee to stay calm as well. By listening carefully and taking your mentee seriously, you will help your mentee to feel safer and more comfortable.
- Determine whether or not your mentee is in immediate danger. You might want to ask your mentee, "Do you feel safe going home/to school/etc. today?"
- Let your mentee know that you are concerned about his or her safety and ask your mentee how you can help: "Would you like me to help you tell your parents?" Often children will not want you to say anything to anyone. But, it is important to let your mentee know that you want to help him or her feel safe and therefore you will need to tell the Program Coordinator(s) or other adults.

- Keep in mind that you may be the first person your mentee feels safe sharing this information with. Or, you may be the first person who really hears and believes them.
- **Contact a Program Coordinator before you take any action. Please call us as soon as you can, and if you can't reach us, contact the principal, school counselor, or your mentee's parents if the matter is urgent. Do not try to handle this alone. (Remember, important phone numbers are listed in the front of this manual.)**

Suspected Abuse:
In the case of suspected abuse (not direct disclosure) it is important that you let a Program Coordinator know immediately. Document suspicions, reasons for suspicion, and any important details.

Emergencies:
If your mentee is in imminent danger, may harm self/other or needs medical help:
1) Call 911 immediately.
2) Call a Program Coordinator as soon as possible.

1. **Remember your mentors.** As you think about your role as a mentor, try to remember people in your own life who may have served as formal or informal mentors to you - people that are older than yourself with whom you have a trusting relationship – an uncle, a coach, parent, or friend who helps you understand yourself better.

2. **Act as an older friend or trusted guide.** The mentor's role is to be a trusted guide and a friend: someone who can help steer you on a better path. You should not try to be like a parent or a teacher, someone who wields power and tries to discipline.

3. **Recognize nobody's perfect.** Nobody's perfect, and everyone is unique. When you are mentoring, the most important thing is to be sincere and offer yourself as a friend. Don't try to play a role or be the perfect mentor. Don't be afraid of making mistakes. And if you make a mistake it is a chance to role model what to do afterwards. Be yourself.

4. **Notice how you communicate with your mentee.** When you talk to your mentee think about whether you are acting and sounding more like a friend, teacher or parent. If your mentee tells you that she hasn't been doing her homework, do you react by lecturing her to think about her future; or do you ask if she needs help?

5. **Embrace difference.** Don't try to change who your mentee is. Hopefully, when you are matched with a mentee you will have some interests in common. But remember that your differences are also part of your relationship. Help your mentee to recognize who he is as an individual. Don't try to make him more like you, and don't compare him to other mentees.

6. **Remember it's OK not to know.** Sometimes your mentee will ask you for advice on a topic you don't know much about. Help your mentee by showing her how to figure out the answer. Don't try to pretend you know everything. You'll help your mentee a lot more by showing her how to find a good solution than by acting like you know everything.

7. **Start with hello.** The way you say "hello" can be a powerful gesture. At the beginning of a meeting, think about how you greet him. Are you enthusiastic and happy to see him? Or do you ignore him because you are talking to someone else? The feeling you give when you say hello can set the tone for the rest of the meeting, and make him feel great.

8. **Be present.** Your most important gift to your mentee is your presence; not just your physical presence, but also your attention. If you miss a meeting, this can be hard on your mentee, and she will worry about whether you like her. If you come to all your meetings but seem distant and distracted, this can also create doubts in your mentee's mind about how much you care.

9. **Provide empathy, praise, and attention.** The most important characteristic of a good mentor is the ability to offer empathy, praise, and attention. As an example, imagine your mentee says he is having trouble in math class. Let him know that you understand how he feels—sometimes we all have trouble grasping certain concepts, and that can be frustrating. Highlight his strengths by praising his unique skills and genuine efforts. Let him know that you are there for him, and if you can help him grasp some problem he's having trouble with, take the time to do so.

10. **Understand you are not a tutor.** While you will probably spend some time helping your mentee with homework, don't try to judge your effectiveness by your mentee's success in school. If your mentee feels you have been a good friend, and helped her to know herself better, that will have longer lasting significance than any improvement in grades.

Adapted and used with permission from Ze'ev Korn's Mentor Training. William (Ze'ev) Korn, MSW, M.Ed., Los Angeles. CA. 2008.

Rapport Building: First Impressions...

Things to Consider Before Meeting with your Mentee

Relationships Take Time

Before you meet with your mentee for the first time, keep in mind that all relationships take time to warm up. Some mentees may seem very open initially, but take time to move toward a deeper relationship. Others may try to test you by pushing you away, seeming disinterested, or acting like they don't want to meet you; but deep down, they want to get to know you. Remember, many of these students have experienced significant losses of parents, relatives, or friends in their lives. Some of their adult role models may be inconsistent in maintaining a relationship with them. It may take several weeks of meeting before your mentee feels they can trust you as a consistent person in their life.

If You Experience Resistance

If you experience resistance or disinterest that you think is more than just "testing the limits" you can always check your assumptions by asking for feedback. Tell them, "I like coming to meet with you each week, and I'd like to continue to meet, but if you really feel like you don't want to meet, you should just let me know. Would it be ok if we continued to meet each week?" And see what kind of response you get.

Use Your Resources

Remember, if you're feeling like the relationship isn't going well, use your support network. Talk to your Program Coordinator or one of the Lead Mentors, ask questions at mentor trainings, and talk to other mentors.

Re-matching Possibilities and Closure

If for some reason your match is not going well and both you and your mentee want to bring it to a close, you should tell the student you will contact the Program Coordinator at your school to discuss this. If it is decided that it's best to close the match, the Program Coordinator at your school will arrange a "closure meeting" (i.e. to discuss ending the match and ensure the child does not feel criticized or rejected). At that point, you may be re-matched or allowed to make another choice based on your program or class requirements. <u>Regardless of how the match ends, however, we follow guidelines in the "Termination Ritual" to make sure it is a good ending for everyone.</u>

Mentee-Mentor Termination Ritual
(created with Kimberley Lakes, Ph.D.)

Termination may be the result of a variety of situations.

♦   Sometimes it may become necessary to terminate a match due to conflicts between the mentee and mentor.
♦   Sometimes termination may occur because either the mentee or the mentor drop out of the program. The dropouts may occur as a result of relationship conflicts or other factors (i.e., mentor's time limitations, or mentor transfers to another school).
♦   Sometimes it may become apparent that the mentee and/or mentor may work more effectively with another mentor/mentee. In these cases, reassignment may be best.
♦   Sometimes it occurs in a planned way, such as at the end of the school year.

Termination should provide closure and opportunities for learning. In order for termination to accomplish this, mentors should follow these guidelines:
♦   Identify and verbally clarify the reasons for termination with your mentee. If the reasons involve the behavior of either you or your mentee, this should be presented in a constructive manner. If your mentee was tardy, skipped meetings, or was disrespectful try to express how this made you feel. If you engaged in any of these behaviors, try to explain that these problems were your fault, and not your mentee's.
♦   Give your mentee the opportunity to discuss with you what worked and didn't work in your relationship and to identify ways to handle future situations more effectively. The Program Coordinator will facilitate a conversation between you and your mentee in order to make sure that you both express yourselves positively and constructively. This information may be critical to successfully re-matching you and/or your mentee.
♦   You and your mentee should share feelings that you each have about ending your relationship. Mentors who are terminating because of time limitations or other reasons not related to the mentee need to make particularly clear to the mentee that s/he did not do anything to make you leave. You should share the things about your mentee that you liked. Without this--and often even with it to a lesser degree--the mentee will feel unlovable or flawed in some way. You should do all that you can to convince the mentee this is not so.

If your mentee leaves the program, do not discuss with other mentors (or mentees!) any personal problems you had with your mentee. If others ask, just let them know that the program wasn't working out for the mentee. Your Program Coordinator should talk to the group about anyone leaving the program or being reassigned, so you shouldn't have to answer too many questions.

Previous mentors have had various hopes and concerns about becoming a mentor. We want to share their thoughts with you for several reasons. First, it's important to know that you are not alone in your worries about whether or not you will be a good mentor, or whether the experience will overwhelm you, or whether it will work out. Those questions are normal. Knowing that most people have similar fears, and that they still go on to have wonderful experiences, may provide reassurance.

Second, it's important to keep your hopes in line with the program goals and with what's realistic. The goal of the program is to help students learn better social interaction skills, and to be more connected to self, others and society. The mentoring relationships provide support for this. Socially adept students like you can serve as role models for behavior. The supportive relationship you provide can help a child feel better about him or herself, or it may lead the child to avoid risk-taking and self-destructive behaviors. But mentors are often disappointed when their primary goals are to "change" others, to "teach good values," or to "tell people how they need to live." The mentors who get the most out of mentoring--and who seem to be most effective--are those who understand the power of friendship, encouragement, and a good shoulder or ear.

Below are two lists of hopes and concerns. These are provided to help you begin to think about your goals. Ask yourself,

- "Are my goals or interests in line with the program's goals?"
- "Do I realize how powerful it could be for a young child to be listened to and cared for?"
- "Can I provide the support to my mentor that others gave to me?"

These questions are the questions of successful mentors. Ask yourself,

- "Do I think my role is to change the child?"
- "Do I think my values and beliefs are right and theirs are wrong?"
- "Do I feel sorry for kids like that?"

These questions usually suggest that the mentor has an agenda--often an arrogant or ignorant one--that will likely interfere with the mentee's need to feel heard, understood, and liked. So think about what makes you want to be a mentor, and decide whether those interests are likely to support or sabotage your work.

Common Hopes

1)   that my mentee keeps coming through the school year
2)   that I can keep the same mentees from last year if we continue
3)   that I get to know my mentee by the end of the program
4)   that I reach out to and "reach" my mentee
5)   that I will be able to make my mentee understand right and wrong
6)   that my mentee and I establish a good, solid relationship
7)   that I learn about myself and my mentee
8)   that I get to know other mentees besides mine
9)   that I and my mentee have fun
10) that my school work does not prevent me from coming this summer
11) that I will be able to bond with other mentors
12) that I will be a good role model
13) that my mentee remembers me for the rest of his/her life
14) that I will learn about childhood from my mentee
15) that I can give as much as necessary
16) that I will give a kid a support system that he/she can depend upon
17) that I will make a positive impact on my mentee
18) that I will get my mentee to open up more
19) that I will give my mentee help academically
20) that I will keep up with my commitments to my mentee

Concerns can be just as instructive and just as important to think about. What are you worried about? Sometimes our worries get in the way of our work. Think about your fears. Then consider whether to share these concerns with your mentee, your peers, or the Program Coordinators. Maybe you just want to be aware of your fears so you can avoid fulfilling them. <u>Have you had any of the following concerns?</u>

Common Concerns
1) that we will be assigned different mentees than the ones from last year
2) that I won't know what to do with the mentee
3) that there won't be enough time to always get together
4) that sports will interfere with me meeting my mentee
5) that my mentee will hate being around me
6) that I won't interact with other kids since I'll only have one mentee
7) that I won't be able to connect with my mentee
8) that the mentees and mentors won't have fun together
9) that my mentee will be hard to reach
10) that I will show favoritism to some of the children
11) that I will not be able to teach my mentee anything
12) that I won't get along with my new mentee
13) that it will be hard to keep the relationship going when I'm at college
14) that my new mentee and old mentee won't get along
15) that I won't be able to keep up with my mentee
16) that the mentee won't be interested in what we plan to do
17) that I won't end up with a mentee
18) that I won't be able to help my mentee
19) that I will neglect to call or meet with my mentee
20) that I will have trouble controlling the mentees
21) that my mentee has problems that I can't solve
22) that I can't fulfill my mentees needs
23) that it will get kind of hard
24) that there will be competition for my attention

Our First Meeting: A Planning Worksheet
(created with Laura Roy-Carlson, Ph.D.)

(This has been updated to match training info)
Basic Background Information

My mentee's name is:

Nickname (if any):

Homeroom Teacher's Name:

Phone number (s):

Email address:

What would I like my mentee to call me?

Thinking about your first meeting: You might want to think about some conversation starters or ice-breaker activities to help get to know your mentee a little better. Review the Rapport Building section of your Mentor Handbook (above) for help.

What are some things I could tell my mentee about myself that would help us get to know each other better? What about me and my life story might be interesting and relevant to this young person?

____

____

____

My mentee will have been told that one or both of us indicated the liked meeting the other person after the meet and greet, and that's why we were paired, but also because we shared interests in sports, music, hobbies, family experiences, favorite classes, etc. So, what might be some of the things you got paired on-- make a list of your interests.

My Interests:

____

____

____

What are some questions I could ask my mentee to get to know her/him without prying?

____

____

____

What do I want out of the mentoring relationship – Summarize your hopes?

____

____

____

How can I find out what my mentee hopes to get out of the relationship – what questions might I ask?

____

____

____

Other things I want to remember for the first day: ____________________

____

____

Ask for what you want assertively by following these steps:

1. Say how you feel, using "I" messages.
2. Respect the other person's feelings, beliefs, intentions and needs. Do this by asking for the other person's perspective on the problem or situation.
3. Decide what you need, and how you can get it in a way that works for both of you and keeps your relationship strong. You can do this by stating a solution that makes you both happy, or that at least does not offend the other person because it shows that you understand his or her needs too (even if those needs don't match your own).

FOUR GOALS OF MISBEHAVIOR[8]

Goals:
To understand why children misbehave and to understand how to use praise and empowerment to prevent misbehavior

When children feel discouraged they misbehave. They do not feel connected in meaningful ways. Therefore, they seek belonging and connectedness through misbehavior.

Children's misbehaviors can be classified into four broad categories or "goals" in the sense that the misbehaviors help a child achieve something.
1. Getting attention
2. Feeling powerful
3. Getting revenge
4. Displaying feelings of inadequacy

These goals are the same throughout life though they may look different in children and adults.

---

[7] Adapted from *From peer pressure to peer support* (p. 231) by Shelley Mackay Freeman.
[8] Adapted from the 1992 PAL's Teacher Manual with permission from Workers' Assistance Programs of Texas, Inc. They reprinted it with permission from American Guidance Service, Publishers Building, Circle Pines, MN 55014. Originally from *Systematic Training for Effective Parenting* by Don Dinkmeyer and Gary D. McKay, 1989.

Although the four goals seem complex at first, we have found that anyone can learn how to discover the purpose of a child's misbehavior by using two simple steps. Remember that since misbehavior serves a purpose, it is best understood by observing its consequences. That is, does the behavior reflect the child's attempts to meet needs for belonging, freedom, or power?

Step 1:
Observe your own reaction to the child's misbehavior. Your feelings point to the child's goals. Ask yourself, "What is this child trying to achieve?" (e.g., if the child's behavior makes you feel provoked and angry, it was probably intended to help the child achieve power over you).

Step 2:
Observe the child's reaction to your attempts at correction. The child's response to your behavior will also let you know what the child is seeking. Everyone wants attention, praise, and support. When these aren't provided children feel frustrated and powerless. As a result they may try to achieve power or even take revenge. Other children feel hopeless and give up trying to get their basic needs met.

Summary: Train yourself to look at the results of misbehavior rather than just at the misbehavior. The results of the misbehavior reveal its purpose.

With these needs and two techniques in mind, let's consider the four goals of misbehavior:

ATTENTION
All people need to receive praise, attention and support from others. The psychoanalysis Kohut (1977)[9] says this is what gives people their self-esteem and ambition. Most children prefer to gain attention and praise in useful ways; but if those ways don't work they seek attention in useless (even destructive) ways. Children who hold the conviction that they can have their need for *belonging* met only if they are receiving constant attention prefer negative attention to being ignored.

When a child is seeking attention in negative ways, you will feel pestered and annoyed. To help attention-seeking children, we must change our responses to show them that they can feel *powerful* and competent through useful contributions rather than through useless bids for attention. We must focus on

---

[9] Kohut, H. (1977). *Restoration of the self.* New York: International Universities Press.

their constructive behavior; we must either ignore the misbehavior or pay attention to it in ways they don't expect. Therefore, try hard to provide praise and attention when your mentee acts appropriately.

Attention should not be given on demand, even for positive acts, because this reinforces inappropriate desire for attention. Children easily come to believe that if they are not "center stage," they are being left out (and do not *belong*).

The helpful way to give attention is to give it when it is not expected. This places emphasis upon giving rather than getting. We realize that at this point, these sound like oversimplified, quick solutions. But for now we are interested only in you really understanding the general idea of how to stop reinforcing misbehavior. So, rather than laughing at goofy or silly behavior or becoming angry at misbehavior, try to praise your mentee in different ways and at times when they are not "standing out" by misbehavior or trying to draw attention to themselves. If you can praise your mentee three times everyday when they are not seeking attention, you will be more effective when you ask your mentee to stop undesirable behavior.

POWER

Power-seeking children feel they are significant only when they are the boss. They might say "No one can force me to do anything" (also an expression of the need for *freedom*) or "You better do what I want." Even if adults do succeed in subduing them, the victory is only temporary. These adults win the argument, but lose the relationships.

The problem is that when a child is defiant, others (even adults) feel angry and provoked. Attempts to correct the child are seldom successful because they are done out of anger and force. The child will defy others and continue the unacceptable behavior (because they are still getting attention and are powerful by controlling others). Or the child will stop temporarily. But in the absence of feeling powerful in other ways, the child likely will continue with more intensity. Some children in power struggles do what they are told, but not in a way that others want it done. We call this "defiant compliance."

As a rule, when dealing with power-seeking children, adults must refrain from getting angry and must disengage themselves from the power struggle. Using power tactics to counter children's bids for power only impresses them with the value of power and increases their desire for power. What helps most is planning, ahead of time, to satisfy the child's need for power, freedom, fun and belonging through planned, constructive opportunities for leadership and participation. Children's need for power can be quenched by (1) allowing them the freedom to make important choices (e.g., about activities); (2) giving them leadership roles in the mentor-mentee pair.

If the struggle for negative displays of power continues and the children come to feel they cannot defeat the adults, they may alter the desire for power and pursue the third goal, revenge.

REVENGE

Children who pursue revenge are convinced that they are not lovable and that they don't belong; that they are significant (and powerful) only when they are able to hurt others as they believe they have been hurt. They find a place and achieve power by being cruel and disliked.

People dealing with the revengeful child feel just like the child feels: deeply hurt and wanting to retaliate. The child responds to their counterattack by seeking further revenge, either by intensifying the misbehavior or by choosing another sort of weapon. These people need to realize that the child's revengeful behavior stems from discouragement and is not necessarily "caused" by the people themselves.

To begin to help the revengeful child, mentors must be on guard not to retaliate. As difficult as it will be, mentors must improve their relationship with their child by remaining calm and showing good will. By showing your mentee that he or she is loveable, important and cared for (even when they misbehave) he or she will not feel attacked. You will be able to discipline or correct behavior in ways that do not provoke vengeful feelings. Even if the child must be removed from the room, asked to sit aside to calm down, or told he or she must go home that day, this must be communicated in a calm, supportive, understanding way that validates the child's worth as a person but makes clear that some behaviors are not acceptable. We want the child to know he or she can decide to act bad or good, rather than feeling an overriding sense of deficiency or inadequacy.

DISPLAY OF INADEQUACY

Children who display inadequacy, or disability, are often extremely discouraged. They have given up hope of succeeding. They attempt to keep others from expecting anything of them. Giving up may be total or only in areas where children feel they can't succeed, such as in academics, socializing, or being creative.

Mentors will know that their mentee is pursuing this goal if they, too, feel despair and want to give up; if they feel like "throwing up their hands." The child responds passively or fails to respond to whatever the mentor does. The child slows the relationship's development.

To help a child who feels inadequate, mentors must eliminate all criticism, and focus, instead, on the mentee's assets and strengths. The mentor must encourage any effort to improve, no matter how small it seems.

Although we presented the four goals of misbehavior in a progression from attention-getting through power, revenge, and display of inadequacy, children may not follow this course, because they select their goals according to their perceptions. For example: a

pampered child who passively seeks attention may progress directly to displaying inadequacy if he or she sees the parents' overprotection as proof of their lack of confidence in the child. Like children who have been abused, pampered children may conclude that they are powerless to overcome the difficulties of life or to be loved by and important to others.

Remember that all misbehavior—even the inappropriate bid for attention—stems from discouragement. The child lacks courage to behave in an active, constructive manner. A child does not misbehave unless he or she feels a real or threatened loss of status. Whatever goal the misbehavior serves, it is done in the belief that the behavior is the only way the child can have a place in the group. We can discover the goal a child seeks only by observing the results. Once we discover the goal, we are in a position to begin redirecting the child through the consistent application of praise, empathy, and attention, and by providing the child real opportunities to create and to succeed.

  p. 39

Although they are often aware of the consequences of their misbehavior, children are usually unaware of their goals.

When your mentee misbehaves, (1) try not to point it out publicly (this provides negative attention), (2) try to divert the child to an activity that provides them power, freedom, fun or a sense of belonging.

To prevent misbehavior, (1) praise your mentee three times a day in non-attention seeking situations, (2) point out his or her skills, talents, and creativity, (3) help your mentee see how good behavior leads attention and affection from others. You can also provide empathy, praise and attention to other mentees as a way of showing what your mentee can expect from you if he or she behaviors in an appropriate manner.

This table will help you determine which type of misbehavior your mentee might be manifesting, and how you should approach the problem:

Goal of Misbehavior	You will feel...	You should react by...
Attention	Annoyed, pestered	Not giving attention "on demand"; praising the child at times when not attention seeking
Power	Angry, provoked	Disengaging from power struggle; empowering child through planned activities
Revenge	Hurt, wanting to retaliate	Expressing problems with child's behavior, while supporting child's self-worth
Display of Inadequacy	Despair, hopelessness	Eliminating criticism; highlighting child's strengths & assets

Constructive Criticism[10]

Objective: Understand how to give constructive criticism.

If you want someone to change a behavior or make a personal improvement, it's important to give criticism or make suggestions in a positive way. Always do these three things:
1. Say something good.
2. Describe the problem.
3. Suggest a solution.

YOUR STYLE OF CONFLICT RESOLUTION[11]

Objective: Determine your style of conflict resolution with the following questionnaire. Although your style may vary from one situation to another, this activity will give you an indication of how you most often choose to solve your conflicts.

Procedure: Conflict Resolution Situation Style: Preparing for a with your Mentee to Yumewii Mountain

Read the following situations and possible solutions and decide which way you would choose to solve the conflict by placing a '1' next to your first choice, a '2' next to your second choice, and so on. Be sure to rank each response from 1 to 5. There are no right or wrong answers. Be sure to mark them the way you actually likely **would** respond, not the way you think people should choose.

Situation A: Nancy has been spreading rumors around the school about you. You've been good friends with her for years and are very hurt that she's telling lies about you.

______ 1. You ignore Nancy and don't bring up the topic when she talks to you.

______ 2. You sit down with Nancy and ask her why she's spreading rumors. She tells you it's because of something you did. Although you don't agree

---

[10] Adapted from *From peer pressure to peer support* (p. 254) by Shelley Mackay Freeman.
[11] Adapted from *From peer pressure to peer support* (p. 246-247) by Shelley Mackay Freeman.

with her, you both try to give a little to mend the hard feelings to keep your friendship strong.

_______ 3. Never admitting you were wrong in any way or that you understand her criticisms of you, you complain to Nancy about how mean she is until Nancy comes over to you and apologizes.

_______ 4. You decide that next time you see Nancy you'll be extra nice to her, give her gifts and compliments, and invite her over to your house so that she'll be nicer to you.

_______ 5. You and Nancy talk about what caused the hard feelings. To strengthen the relationship, you both come up with several things that you both can to do next time so misunderstandings like this don't happen again.

Situation B: You've played basketball since second grade and think you're pretty good. But the varsity coach is making you sit on the bench for most of the games.

_______ 6. You ask the coach why you aren't playing more, and in response you play up the coach's desire to win and suggest if you played more the team would win more. Then the two of you decide how you could can play more.

_______ 7. You change the subject every time your parents ask you why you aren't playing more during the games.

_______ 8. You tell the Athletic Director that your coach is unfair and should be fired because he chooses favorites to play.

_______ 9. You ask the coach if he'll let you play more the next game since you practiced extra hours at home this week. He says no, and you accept his stand on the issue to avoid any more conflict.

_______ 10. You help the coach put away all the equipment after the game and offer to figure out all the statistics for the game even though you didn't play.

Situation C: Your friend Arnie is having a keg party at his house because his parents are gone. He's angry at you because you say you won't be coming. You're angry at him for drinking and lying to his parents.

_______ 11. You tell Arnie that you'll come for a little while, but you won't drink.

_______ 12. You and Arnie try to figure out several activities for that night that you both enjoy doing without drinking.

_______ 13. You tell Arnie you have to go out of town with your family.

_______ 14. You have your own party and get all the friends who would be going to Arnie's party to come to your part. That way, he has to come to your party to see the other friends.

_______ 15. You go to the party and pretend to drink to make Arnie happy.

Total up your scores in the columns below. Look at the total scores to determine which style of conflict resolution (Avoiding, Smoothing, Compromising, Forcing, and Problem Solving) you use most often.

	Avoiding (Turtle) Level 0	Soothing & Complying (Teddy Bear)	Compromise to get your needs met Fox or Dove	Forcing (Shark) or Resisting (Donkey)	Problem Solving & Collaborating by creating new shared goals (Owl)
Situation A	1.	4.	2.	3.	5.
Situation B	7.	10.	9.	8.	6.
Situation C	13.	15.	11.	14.	12.
Totals					

Each style is appropriate sometimes. But usually the best way to get at the root of a conflict is to use the "problem-solving" style. Sometimes there is no solution that makes everyone happy; in these cases it may be necessary to use another style of conflict resolution, such as compromising. But it's always good to begin with the problem solving style, and then try something else if that doesn't work.

When talking with your mentee or planning activities, consider what you can do to help your mentee learn to resolve conflicts using the compromising or collaborating problem-solving style. Ask questions that get to the root of a conflict, help them practice finding solutions that directly address the problem without ignoring anyone's needs.

Also note that how we choose to resolve conflicts often reflects
> what we've learned from people around us,
> how safe we feel in a specific situation
> our religious or moral feelings about topics
> and our cultural beliefs about relationships (with peers and adults)*

So, be sensitive to the possible role of (non-developmental) factors as well.

* Keller calls these horizontal (equally power = peers) and vertical (differential power = child-parent or child-teacher relationships).

PROBLEM-SOLVING STEPS[12]

Objective:
Practicing structured problem-solving techniques from the different perspectives of the perspective-taking levels (Selman's model), the styles of conflict resolution animals (Johnson's model, above), or in terms of specific social skills required in solving problems.

Procedure: Imagine a problem and work through the steps described below.

1. Define the problem or conflict.

2. Analyze the problem or conflict.
List things that could make the situation worse and those that could make it better.

Hurting factors	Helping factors
_______________________	_______________________
_______________________	_______________________
_______________________	_______________________

3. List possible solutions.
From the list of helping factors above, choose possible solutions. Gather more information if necessary.

4. Choose a solution.
Write down what results you would expect from it.

5. Evaluate.
Do you think it's a good solution? Go back to steps #3 and #4 if necessary.

---

[12] Adapted from *From peer pressure to peer support* (p. 248) by Shelley Mackay Freeman.

There will be times when your mentee has a problem that reflects an exaggerated view of a situation or view of him or herself. This is not a huge problem that requires adult intervention, such as if physical abuse, violence, or drug use was involved. And it is not a problem that reflects their misbehavior, which we will cover in the next set of activities. Rather, in this case their problem is something that is not going well in his or her life, about which your mentee has concerns and is worried, anxious or sad. These are different than the problems addressed earlier by problem solving techniques. In those problems, there typically were specific circumstances or relationships where problems were happening and for which one or another alternative response would solve the problem.

Here we are talking about problems that the child feels are more "pervasive," meaning that the child thinks there is something wrong with them "all the time," or that something "always" happens or "never" goes his or her way. It might be something like one of the following:
"Other kids never want to play with me."
"None of my teachers like me."
"I always fail my tests."
"I feel really sad and alone."

One way to help a person is to use the solution-focused approach when listening to them and as a way of being supportive. This is a good approach because it does not require you to ask personal questions about the child's family or background. It also allows you to empower or encourage your mentee to take charge of solving his or her own problem. There are two key principles to keep in mind when using this technique:

1. The mentee knows best: Assuming this, determine: (a) How your mentee see the problem? (b) How has the mentee tried to solve the problem in the past? And (c) why does he or she feel those attempts at problem solving did not work?

2. If at first you don't succeed try something different: Difficulties become problems when they are mishandled by applying the same unhelpful solution again

---

[13] Based on Duncan, B. L. and Murphy, J. J. (2007). *Brief interventions for school problems.* New York: Guilford.

and again. Sometimes how your mentee has solved a similar problem will provide the answer.

Try two things: Problem busting and Solution building.

Problem-busting

Problem-busting encourages the your mentee to change the way she approaches the problem by (a) getting multiple perspectives on the problem from different people, (b) recognizing patterns involved in problems by helping him or her see similarities across different people's perspectives on the problems, and then (c) encouraging fresh new strategies. For this to work, you will need to ask your mentee to do some research. Namely, have the mentee go ask peers, parents, friends, teachers, and anyone else why they think your mentee is having that problem. Then have your mentee report back to you what they learned. With this information, the problem might look different or get resolved altogether. Sometimes, if you help your mentee ask the right questions, the problem will take care of itself. Or, it might provide the information you need to do some solution building.

Solution building:

Elicit exceptions and draw attention to them. Here you find those times when the problem was not present. For example, when kids *did* want to play with your mentee, when a teacher *did* like him or her, when he or she *did well* on a test, or felt happy instead of sad. These are the exceptions to the problem. Once you identify a few exceptions, you can find out why, when or how those exceptions took place.

Elaborate exceptions. Get all the details you can. When listening to responses to these questions, listen for the "heroic mentee." Listen for heroic stories, those that point out times when your mentee had success in overcoming similar problems in other relationships or situations. Sometimes, a skill or strength that helped solve a different problem can be applied to the present problem in some manner.

Expand exceptions. Then, think about how whatever allowed those exceptions to happen could be expanded to the current problem or applied to it. The child may have acted in a different way at times when the problem was not there. He or she might have had a different attitude—more hopeful, confident or less frightened. Or, elaborating the exceptions might point to particular relationships or contexts where your mentee is more successful (e.g., the problem always arises around some particular friends of hers), so you suggest she spends more time in those places or with those people where the problem does not occur.

SOCIAL PERSPECTIVE TAKING LEVELS
AND THE
INTERPERSONAL NEGOTIATION STRATEGIES (INS)[14]
EACH LEVEL SUPPORTS

PERSPECTIVE-TAKING: INS

EXAMPLES OF INS FOR THE TWO

INTERPERSONAL ORIENTATIONS

	Self-transforming	**Other-transforming**
3rd-person: Collaborative	Collaboration; acting out of shared needs & concern for "us." Here actions are considered for their effects on the relationship; the "we" perspective is given primacy over individual perspectives.	
2nd-person: Cooperative ("self-reflective")	Ask why, barter, go second ⟷	Argue, persuade, go first
1st-person: Unilateral or One-way ("subjective")	Obey, give in, acquiesce ⟷	Dictate, bully, order, tell
Egocentric: Impulsive	Whine, flee, hide ⟷	Fight, grab, hit

Other- vs. Self-Transforming Styles

compromise 3) Mutual *compromise*
Collaboration

persuasion 2) Self-reflective *deference*
(more take) Cooperation (more give)

order 1) Subjective *obey*
(all take) One-way strategies (all give)

"fight" 0) Egocentric *"flight"*
Impulsivity

---

[14] Based on Selman, R. L., & Schultz, L. H. (1990). *Making a friend in youth: Developmental theory and pair therapy.* Chicago: University of Chicago Press.

Resolving Interpersonal Conflict

Conflict Strategies: What are you like?

Level INS – Self-Transforming

The Turtle (Withdrawing). Turtles withdraw into their shells to avoid conflicts. They give up their personal goals and relationships. They stay away from the issues over which the conflict is taking place and from the people they are in conflict with.

Level INS – Other-Transforming

The Shark (Forcing). Sharks try to overpower opponents by forcing them to accept their solutions to the conflict. Their goals are highly important to them, and the relationships is of minor importance. Sharks assume that conflicts are settled by one person winning and one person losing. They want to be the winner.

Level INS – Self -Transforming

The Teddy Bear (Soothing). To Teddy Bears, the relationship is of great importance, while their own goals are of little importance. They want to be accepted and liked by other people. They think that conflict should be avoided in favor of harmony and believe that conflicts cannot be discussed without damaging relationships. Teddy Bears give up their goals to preserve the relationship.

Level INS – Other-Transforming

The Fox (Compromising). Foxes are moderately concerned with their own goals and about their relationships with other people. Foxes seek a compromise. They give up part of their goals and persuade the other person in a conflict to give up part of his goals. They seek a solution to conflicts by which both side gain something. They are willing to sacrifice part of their goals and relationships in order to find agreement for the common good.

Level INS

The Owl (Confronting). Owls highly value their own goals and relationships. They view conflict as problems to be solved and seek a solution that achieves both their own goals and the goals of the other person in the conflict. Owls see conflicts as improving relationships by reducing tension between two people. They try to begin a discussion that identifies the conflict as a problem. Be seeking solutions that satisfy both themselves and the other person, owls maintain the relationship.

Adapted from "Reaching Out: Interpersonal Effectiveness and Self-Actualization", Prentice Hall, 1990; by David W. Johnson & "Making A Friend in Youth", Aldine De Gruyter, 1990; by Robert L. Selman & Lynn H. Schultz

We think these styles of relating are closely tied to the developmental levels of perspective-taking. Understanding how such common interpersonal negotiation strategies often are related to your mentees' underlying perspective-taking abilities may help you think about the best way to encourage them to "move up the developmental ladder."

What is the style of negotiation your mentee most often enlists?

So, what is the next level up the developmental level for your mentee then?

Finally, what can you do to help foster your mentee's perspective-taking skills, and thereby promote their use of more mature or complex negotiation strategies.
For fun, which style might your friends or your parent(s) say you are most likely to use? (The point, how we interact is not only a function of our perspective-taking skills. Often we are just different in ways that also shapes how we relate to others).

The Owl (Confronting).

Level INS – Level 3 (neither Self – nor Other –Transforming)
Owls highly value their own goals and relationships. They view conflict as problems to be solved and seek a solution that achieves both their own goals and the goals of the other person in the conflict. Owls see conflicts as improving relationships by reducing tension between two people. They try to begin a discussion that identifies the conflict as a problem. Be seeking solutions that satisfy both themselves and the other person, owls maintain the relationship.

The Fox (Compromising yet manipulating).

Level 2 INS – Other –Transforming
Foxes are moderately concerned with their own goals and about their relationships with other people. Foxes seek a compromise, but always a self-serving one. They give up part of their goals and persuade the other person in a conflict to give up part of his goals. They seek a solution to conflicts by which both side gain something. They are willing to sacrifice part of their goals and relationships in order to find agreement for the common good but always prioritize their gains.

The *Dove* (Peacemaker).

Level 2 INS –Self –Transforming
To Doves are flexible, understanding, considerate, and open to others' needs. But their unique, individual needs, desires, and interests take a back seat. They will try to talk out problems, have a "meeting of the minds," but in the end typically comply to keep others happy.

The *Donkey* (Resisting).

Level 1 INS – Other -Transforming
Donkeys state their point of view—what they want, need, believe—and don't budge an inch. They resist change until others comply and go along with them. They transform others by being stubborn.

The Teddy Bear (Soothing).

Level 1 INS – Self-Transforming[15] To Teddy Bears, the relationship is of great importance, while their own goals are of little importance. They want to be accepted and liked by other people. They think that conflict should be avoided in favor of harmony and believe that conflicts cannot be discussed without damaging relationships. Teddy Bears give up their goals to preserve the relationship.

The Shark (Forcing).

Level 0 INS Other –Transforming

Sharks try to overpower opponents by forcing them to accept their solutions to the conflict. Their goals are highly important to them, and the relationships is of minor importance. Sharks assume that conflicts are settled by one person winning and one person losing. They want to be the winner.

The Turtle (Withdrawing).

Level 0 INS – Self –Transforming

Turtles withdraw into their shells to avoid conflicts. They give up their personal goals and relationships. They stay away from the issues over which the conflict is taking place and from the people they are in conflict with.

Explain who you see that tend to act like one or more of these animals *(and try to use the self-and other-transforming terms and the perspective-taking levels in your answers)*

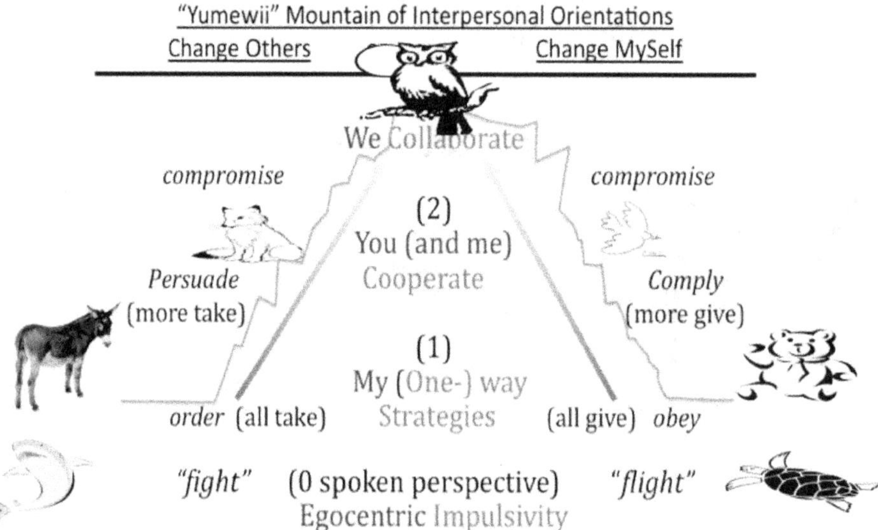

---

[15] Animal names adapted from David W. Johnson (1990) Reaching Out: Interpersonal Effectiveness and Self-Actualization. New York: Prentice Hall.

Sullivan's Developmental Stages Vis-à-vis Mentee Age Groups:

Children (age 4 -8 yr. olds) need to have an adult audience to attend to their play and notice achievements (Many mentees will still need this from their mentors and peers). We'll describe this as the need for "Empathy, Praise, and Attention" later in the training.

Juveniles (age 9-10 yr. olds) need help to manage competition, cooperation, and compromise. Many mentees will not have totally refined these skills yet and need help. They will be identifying their unique skills and abilities, and need to be encouraged to try new things, and appreciate praise for their successes.

Preadolescents (11 & 13 yr. olds) seek out a non-sexual (typically same-sex) confidant, a chum or intimate and are looking to spend time with those whom they shares interests and beliefs. They will start forming in- out-groups. May need help entering groups (avoiding being left out) or venturing outside of their dyads. So structuring group interactions can be very helpful.

Adolescents (14 & 17 year olds) want to discover who they are uniquely and may want to find a sexually intimate (ultimately, a collaborative and loving relationship). Romantic behaviors may be awkward and uncomfortable and self-assessments may be critical and embarrassing. However, socially teens are starting to see how their interests, beliefs, and activity choices result in group memberships. This "group" mentality can be harnessed to create a cohesive program culture, or left alone may result in superficial groupings in the program and even misbehavior. Trying to help mentors think about their beliefs, share and discuss them, is one unique important goal of training.

APPENDIX: Problem Behaviors--Anticipating and Preventing Them

Best way to orient the Match around a set of positive rules

1. Limit rules to four to six, so they may be remembered. Generate them together.
2. Phrase rules in the positive (to do) rather than (don't do). Identify the reason for each.
3. Refer to specific observable behavior (*Hands to yourself*) so it is clear when it is occurring
4. Immediate positive consequences for following rules (praise and rewards of free time), and negative consequences (private reprimand, brief time outs) for rule violations. (No shaming)

Don't let your behavior corrupt your mentees

Minimize the possibility of negative effects resulting from your behavior by making sure you aren't engaging in "deviancy training" (Dishion, McCord, & Poulin, 1999). This can occur when Mentors act out, model, or reinforce delinquent or authority-undermining behaviors. For example, when a mentor suggests to a mentee "Hey, this activity is stupid, let's go see who is hanging out in the hallway" or when a Mentor, if given unstructured time to interact with her same age peers, talks about her romancing or drinking over summer break or on the weekend while her mentee overhears.

Figure 1: Keller's model of relationship dimensions: Where is the mentor?

	(obligation)	(mutual)
Unequal social power/influei (vertical)	***Parent*** ***Teacher*** ***Boss***	***Mentor***
Equal social power/influei (horizontal)	***Cousin***	***Friend*** ***Peer*** ***Partner***

FROM: Laursen, B., & Bukowski, W. M. (1997). A developmental guide to the organization of close relationships. *International Journal of Behavioral Development*, 21(4), 747-770.

(Adapted from *Parent Management Training* by Alan E. Kazdin)

Giving Commands and Instructions: Just as positive opposites make a positive behavior more likely, so do prompts. **A prompt** is a cue or direction we give to get someone to do a behavior.

First, select the desired behavior (positive opposite of misbehavior)

Be specific. Tell you mentee specifically what you want.
Use statement form. Examples: *Poor* / <u>Better</u>
    Poor: "Pick up your stuff." VS.
    Better: "<u>Please pick up the materials you used and put them back.</u>"

Be calm. Keep a positive or neutral tone in your voice, and give a prompt when you enter a situation where behavior is expected
    Poor: "Don't fool around." VS
    Better: "<u>When we're with other kids, remember to keep your hands to yourself and stay in your seat.</u>"

Be close. Go up to your mentee and make eye contact.

Prompt for a behavior no more than twice. Three prompts for the same behavior is nagging.

If the instruction is related to some desired outcome, prompt first: "<u>Now we have a chance to do X (e.g., spend time with peers).</u>" Then state the instruction. Warn once ("Remember, hands to yourself."): if noncompliance results, state: "<u>I'm sorry you chose not to X, we will have other chances to do (the fun thing or desired outcome: e.g., play with peers) next time we meet.</u>"

.

Whenever you want to change behavior, focus on the <u>positive opposite</u>. The positive opposite is the key to increasing positive behavior, and every problem behavior has a positive opposite. It is the behavior you want your child to be doing instead of the negative behavior. . . . Your mentee is more likely to do the positive behavior if given the positive opposite than if punished.

Problem behavior and their Positive Opposites

Not minding	Minding
Yelling . . . when told "no"	Calmly accepting being told "no"
Teasing	Talking nicely
Fighting	Playing cooperatively

What are some examples of positive opposites in peer mentoring?

Effective discipline begins with rewarding and praising positive behaviors. When faced with a problem behavior, mild negative consequences can be effective when paired with (and follow) positive reinforcement for the *positive opposite* of the problem behavior.

An example of an effective discipline technique is **time away**. When used consistently, time out has proven to be quite effective. . . . The mentee leaves the context where the misbehavior is happening to go to a non-reinforcing place for a brief period of time immediately after a problem behavior occurs. But this is not a punishment. Rather, this is simply time "away from the situation" (e.g., the peers, games, desired object) that evoked the misbehavior. Even if your program does not use this approach to behavior management, mentors should know the purpose of time outs (in case they try to use them anyway).

Effective discipline guidelines

1. Remain calm. Focus on the behavior, not on the "mentee" as the problem, and remain supportive of the mentee. Tell the mentee, "I'm sorry you did not X, next time I hope you will do (expected behavior)." Also, if the behavior is occurring, provide a choice, and share that by choosing the misbehavior, the mentee will be choosing to take some cool-down time or to lose a privilege.

2. Use a "time away" to *immediately* remove the mentee from the current context so that your mentee doesn't have the opportunity to engage in more misbehavior. This is just a "cool-down" time—and probably should be called time away, not "time out"

3. If you need to take a privilege away, take it away for a short period of time, such as amount of play time on an afternoon. Have it be known in advance that misbehavior results in the loss of the privilege. How immediate and consistent the consequence is most important. Never withdraw a privilege that is larger than the "crime."

4. Then, praise and reinforce mentee's positive behaviors, such as their compliance with the cool-down time or cooperation with the loss of the privilege. Always be positive and encouraging that the next time the Little will comply with the expected behavior. Be sincere in your expectation that the mentee will be successful in the future.

Positive reinforcement is the most powerful and useful method of changing or developing behaviors. . . . Reinforcement is very familiar to everyone, but it is not used as often as it should be. In fact, if you master the use of positive reinforcement with [your mentee], you will notice really dramatic improvements in behavior. The difficulty is in knowing how to use reinforcement and then in actually using it. Unfortunately, good behavior is usually ignored by adults. Often high five, verbal praise, or the mentor's excitement is all you need.

How to make your praise most effective

  1. **Deliver praise when you are near your mentee.** When you are close to your mentee, you can be sure that the behavior you are praising is taking place. Also, when you are close, your mentee is more likely to pay attention to what you are saying.

  2. **Use a sincere, enthusiastic tone of voice.** You don't need to be loud, but make sure that you sound thrilled about what your mentee does.

  3. **Use nonverbal reinforcers.** Show your mentee you are pleased by smiling, winking, or cheering. Sometimes touch, such as a high five or pat him on the back, will be appropriate, but not always. Make sure your little is okay with such non-verbal communication by asking them if it is okay to, for example, pat him or her on the back, but also watch for any signs that such contact makes the mentee feel uncomfortable. If you sense it might, refrain from doing it further.

  4. **Be specific.** When praising your mentee, say exactly what behavior you approve of. "Wow, thank you so much for picking up your materials and putting them back in the closet."

Name/Number: ________________   Date: ___________
Sex: *Male*___ *Female*__ **Grade:** ___ **Age:** ____

Race/ ethnicity: White__ Black__ Hispanic__ Asian__ Bi-racial__ Native American__ Other: _______

Who do you live with? ◯ mother   ◯ father ______   ◯both   ◯ other: ____________

Do you have siblings (a brother or sister)? ◯ yes   ◯ no (If no, don't answer sibling questions)

Please use this survey to tell us about yourself. Read each statement. CIRCLE the number that best describes how true that statement is for you or how much you agree with it. If a statement is unclear to you, ask for an explanation. If it still unclear, put a " ?".

"How TRUE about you is each sentence?"
Not at all = 1   **Not really = 2**   **Sort of true = 3**   **True = 4**   **Very true = 5**

	Not at all	Not really	Sort of	True	Very true
(1) I like hanging out around where I live (like my neighborhood).	1	2	3	4	5
(2) Spending time with friends is not so important to me.	1	2	3	4	5
(3) I can name 5 things that my friends like about me.	1	2	3	4	5
(4) My family has fun together.	1	2	3	4	5
(5) I have a lot of fun with my brother(s) or sister(s). (leave blank if you have none.)	1	2	3	4	5
(6) I work hard at school.	1	2	3	4	5
(7) My classmates often bother me.	1	2	3	4	5
(8) I care what my teachers think of me.	1	2	3	4	5
(9) I will have a good future.	1	2	3	4	5
(10) I enjoy spending time by myself reading.	1	2	3	4	5

	Not at all	Not really	Sort of	True	Very true
(11) I spend a lot of time with kids around where I live.	1	2	3	4	5
(12) I have friends I'm really close to and trust completely.	1	2	3	4	5
(13) There is not much that is unique or special about me.	1	2	3	4	5
(14) It is important that my parents trust me.	1	2	3	4	5
(15) I feel close to my brother(s) or sister(s). (leave blank if you have none.)	1	2	3	4	5
(16) I enjoy being at school.	1	2	3	4	5

Not at all Not really Sort of True Very true

Not at all Not really Sort of True Very true

(17) I like pretty much all of the other kids in my grade.   1 2 3 4 5

(18) I do not get along with some of my teachers.   1 2 3 4 5

(19) Doing well in school will help me in the future.   1 2 3 4 5

(20) I like to read.   1 2 3 4 5

(21) I get along with the kids in my neighborhood.   1 2 3 4 5

(22) Spending time with my friends is a big part of my life.   1 2 3 4 5

(23) I can name 3 things that other kids like about me.   1 2 3 4 5

(24) I enjoy spending time with my parents.   1 2 3 4 5

(25) I enjoy spending time with my brothers/sisters.   1 2 3 4 5

(leave blank if you have none.)

(26) I get bored in school a lot.   1 2 3 4 5

(27) I like working with my classmates.   1 2 3 4 5

(28) I want to be respected by my teachers.   1 2 3 4 5

(29) I do things outside of school to prepare for my future.   1 2 3 4 5

(30) I never read books in my free time.   1 2 3 4 5

(31) I often spend time playing or doing things in my neighborhood.   1 2 3 4 5

(32) My friends and I talk openly with each other about personal things.   1 2 3 4 5

(33) I really like who I am.   1 2 3 4 5

Not at all Not really Sort of True Very true

(34) My parents and I disagree about many things.   1 2 3 4 5

(35) I try to spend time with my brothers/sisters when I can.   1 2 3 4 5

(36) I do well in school.   1 2 3 4 5

(37) I get along well with the other students in my classes.   1 2 3 4 5

(38) I try to get along with my teachers.   1 2 3 4 5

(39) I do lots of things to prepare for my future.   1 2 3 4 5

(40) I often read when I have free time.   1 2 3 4 5

(41) I hang out a lot with kids in my neighborhood.   1 2 3 4 5

(42) I spend as much time as I can with my friends.   1 2 3 4 5

(43) I have special hobbies, skills, or talents.   1 2 3 4 5

(44) My parents and I get along well.   1 2 3 4 5

Not at all Not really Sort of True Very true

	Not at all	Not really	Sort of	True	Very true
(45) I try to avoid being around my brother/sister(s).	1	2	3	4	5
(leave blank if you have none.)					
(46) I feel good about myself when I am at school.	1	2	3	4	5
(47) I am liked by my classmates.	1	2	3	4	5
(48) I always try hard to earn my teachers' trust.	1	2	3	4	5
(49) I think about my future often.	1	2	3	4	5
(50) I usually like my teachers.	1	2	3	4	5
(51) My neighborhood is boring.	1	2	3	4	5
(52) My friends and I spend a lot of time talking about things.	1	2	3	4	5
(53) I have unique interests or skills that make me interesting.	1	2	3	4	5
(54) I care about my parents very much.	1	2	3	4	5
(55) What I do now will not affect my future.	1	2	3	4	5
(56) Doing well in school is important to me.	1	2	3	4	5
(57) I rarely fight or argue with the other kids at school.	1	2	3	4	5

(Leave **mother** or **father** blank if deceased. If living with a relative/guardian, answer using **mother** ?s)

	Not at all	Not really	Sort of	True	Very true
(58) I enjoy spending time with my father.	1	2	3	4	5
(59) I enjoy spending time with my mother.	1	2	3	4	5
(60) I like getting to know kids from other cultural or racial groups.	1	2	3	4	5
(61) I spend a lot of time with a boyfriend/girlfriend.	1	2	3	4	5
(62) My religion is very important to me.	1	2	3	4	5
(63) My mother and I are pretty close.	1	2	3	4	5
(64) My father and I are pretty close.	1	2	3	4	5
(65) I would like to know more people from different cultural groups.	1	2	3	4	5
(66) I have a boyfriend/girlfriend who is very important to me.	1	2	3	4	5
(67) My father cares a lot about me.	1	2	3	4	5
(68) My mother cares a lot about me.	1	2	3	4	5
(69) I like getting to know people who are culturally different from me.	1	2	3	4	5
(70) I don't really care about having a boyfriend/girlfriend.	1	2	3	4	5
(71) I attend a religious service (like church) regularly.	1	2	3	4	5
(72) My father and I argue a lot.	1	2	3	4	5

	Not at all	Not really	Sort of	True	Very true
(73) My mother and I argue a lot.	1	2	3	4	5
(74) I share my worries and concerns with a boyfriend/girlfriend.	1	2	3	4	5
(75) I am a religious or faithful person.	1	2	3	4	5
(76) I spend as much time as I can with a girlfriend/boyfriend.	1	2	3	4	5
(77) I talk with my mother about very personal things and my problems.	1	2	3	4	5
(78) I talk with my father about very personal things and my problems.	1	2	3	4	5

Next, choose the description from each pair that best reflects what best explains who you would rather be. For each pair of personal characteristics or traits, select the trait which you value more highly. In making each choice, ask yourself which of the traits in that pair you would rather possess as one of your own characteristics. For example, the first pair is "imaginative—rational." If you had to make a choice, which would you rather be?

"I would rather be…"

Imaginative	or	rational
Helpful	or	quick-witted
Neat	or	sympathetic
Level-headed	or	efficient
Intelligent	or	considerate
Self-reliant	or	ambitious
Respectful	or	original
Creative	or	sensible
Generous	or	individualistic
Responsible	or	original
Capable	or	tolerant
Trustworthy	or	wise
Neat	or	logical
Forgiving	or	gentle
Efficient	or	respectful
Practical	or	self-confident
Capable	or	independent
Alert	or	cooperative
Imaginative	or	helpful
Realistic	or	moral
Considerate	or	wise
Sympathetic	or	individualistic
Ambitious	or	patient
Reasonable	or	quick-witted

References: For additional information on CAMP and connectedness

Journal Articles, available through your nearest university library:

Karcher, M. J. (2009). Increases in academic connectedness and self-esteem among high school students who serve as cross-age peer mentors. *Professional School Counseling.*

Karcher, M. J. & Sass, D. (2009). A multicultural assessment of adolescent connectedness: Testing theoretical models for factor equivalence across gender and ethnicity. *Journal of Counseling Psychology.*

Karcher, M. J. (2008). The Cross-age Mentoring Program (CAMP): A developmental intervention for promoting students' connectedness across grade levels. *Professional School Counseling* (slated for Dec. 2008 publication date).

Karcher, M. J. (2008). The Study of Mentoring in the Learning Environment (SMILE): A randomized evaluation of the effectiveness of school-based mentoring. *Prevention Science, 9(2),* 99-113.

Karcher, M. J. & Herrera, C. (2007). School-based mentoring. *Youth Mentoring: Research in Action,* 1(6), 3-16.

Karcher, M. J. (2007). Cross-age peer mentoring. *Youth Mentoring: Research in Action,* 1(7), 3-17.

Karcher, M. J., Kuperminc, G., Portwood, S., Sipe, C., & Taylor, A. (2006). Mentoring programs: A framework to inform program development, research, and evaluation. *Journal of Community Psychology, 34,* 709-725.

Karcher, M. J. & L. Finn. (2005). How connectedness contributes to experimental smoking among rural youth: Developmental and ecological analyses. *Journal of Primary Prevention, 26,* 25-36.

Karcher, M. J. (2005). The effects of school-based developmental mentoring and mentors' attendance on mentees' self-esteem, behavior, and connectedness. *Psychology in the Schools, 42,* 65-77.

Karcher, M. J., Nakkula, M. J., Harris, J. (2005). Developmental mentoring match characteristics: The effects of mentors' efficacy and mentees' emotional support seeking on the perceived quality of mentoring relationships. *Journal of Primary Prevention, 26,* 93-110.

Karcher, M. J., & Lindwall, J. (2003). Social interest, connectedness, and challenging experiences. What makes high school mentors persist? *Journal of Individual Psychology, 59*, 293-315.

Karcher, M. J. (2003). The Hemingway: Measure of Adolescent Connectedness: Validation studies. *ERIC no. ED477969; ERIC/CASS no. CG032433.* http://www.eric.ed.gov/ERICDocs/data/ericdocs2sql/content_storage_01/00 00019b/80/1b/2c/dd.pdf

Karcher, M. J. (2002). The cycle of violence and disconnection among rural middle school students: Teacher disconnection as a consequence of violence. *The Journal of School Violence, 1*, 35-51.

Karcher, M. J., Davis, C., & Powell, B. (2002). The effects of developmental mentoring on connectedness and academic achievement. *The School Community Journal, 12*, 36-50.*

Karcher, M. J, & Lee, Y. (2002). Connectedness among Taiwanese middle school students: A validation study of the Hemingway Measure of Adolescent Connectedness. *Asia Pacific Education Review, 3*(1), 95-114.

Book chapters on CAMP and connectedness:

Karcher, M. J., Holcomb, M. & Zambrano, E. (2008). Measuring adolescent connectedness: A guide for school-based assessment and program evaluation. In H. L. K. Coleman & C. Yeh (Eds.), *Handbook of School Counseling* (pp. 649-669). Mahwah: Lawrence Erlbaum.

Karcher, M. J. (2006). What happens when high school mentors don't show up? In L. Golden. & P. Henderson (Eds.), *Case studies in school counseling* (pp. 44-53). Alexandria, VA: ACA Press.

Karcher, M. J., Roy-Carlson, L., Allen, C., & Gil-Hernandez, D. (2005). Mentoring. In S. Lee (Ed.), *Encyclopedia of school psychology* (pp. 323-326). Thousand Oaks, CA: Sage.

DuBois, D. L. & Karcher, M. J. (2005). Youth mentoring: Theory, research, and practice. In D. L. DuBois, & M. J. Karcher (Eds.), *Handbook of youth mentoring* (pp. 2-11). Thousand Oaks, CA: Sage Publications.

Karcher, M. J. (2005). Cross-age peer mentoring. In D. L. DuBois, & M. J. Karcher (Eds.), *Handbook of youth mentoring* (pp. 266-285). Thousand Oaks, CA: Sage Publications.

Karcher, M. J. (2004). Connectedness and school violence: A framework for developmental interventions. In E. Gerler (Ed.), *Handbook of school violence* (pp. 7-42). Binghamton, NY: Haworth Press.

Karcher, M. J., Brown, B. B., & Elliot, D. (2003). Enlisting peers in developmental interventions: Principles and practices. In S. F. Hamilton & M. A. Hamilton (Eds.), *Handbook of youth development* (pp. 193-215). Thousand Oaks, CA: Sage Publications.